Old Fashioned Song Lyrics

Joseph Hart

ISBN: 978-81-19228-68-3

First Edition: 2023
Rs. 200/-

Cyberwit.net
HIG 45 Kaushambi Kunj, Kalindipuram
Allahabad - 211011 (U.P.) India
http://www.cyberwit.net
Tel: +(91) 9415091004
E-mail: info@cyberwit.net

For David in NYC - he won’t remember me,

but he wrote the music for our songs.

Contents

The Reluctant Exhibitionist

His buddies call him Rover.
Before we moved from Dover
For eight weeks the neighbors held us over.
And I said, "This had better be love."

We fumbled and we panted
And took it all for granted,
But we left Judith Crist "enchanted".
And I said, "This had better be love."

His buddies to a guy were
Impressed when he and I were
Reviewed in The National Enquirer.
And I said, "This had better be love."

And thanks to his clinicians
With similar ambitions
We now reach eleven new positions.
And I said, "This had better be love."

NYC/1970

Sherridan Whiteside's Song

The Countess came from Typangu.
I took her to The Purple Shoe,
A little nook she'd overlook
Because it's in no tourist book.
It's Percy's place. The boy's a whiz
But not the man his sister is.
And thereupon the Countess flew
Directly back to Typangu.
Sherridan not wisely loved,
But loved too well.

We saw Stravinsky's "Rite of Spring",
A rather hectic night of spring,
A most alarming song of spring,
It should be called "The Wrong of Spring".
The cellos swept. The trumpets soared.
But peacefully she slept and snored.
And when the whole ballet was done
I had to say the trumpets won.
Sherridan not wisely loved,
But loved too well.

NYC/1970

Frankie Addams' Song, a fragment

In the apse
A couple of chaps
Will sing us a rhapsody.
Perhaps they'll get a fee.

I assume
That she and the groom
Are able to spawn the kin,
So where do you fit in?

NYC/1970

"Come And Tell Me"

Rodgers & Hart

If you think you could content a
Girl who's lovely in magenta,
You may sit and tell me.
If your fancy vaguely traces
Half remembered names and faces,
You may sit and tell me.
Such a pretty hand
So gentle and so fine.
It's so large that one of yours
Holds both of mine.
If you feel a faint affection
That must not escape detection,
Sit there and tell it to me.

Underneath a quilt
We will be safe and warm,
Snuggled like two children
Hiding from a storm.

NYC/1970

"Let's Do It"

(after Cole Porter)

1.

White mice with rapturous squeaks do it
Plumbers after plugging up your leaks do it
Let's do it
Let's fall in love
Great thinkers sit and ask why do it
Often maiden aunties on the sly do it
Let's do it
Let's fall in love
The penguins far out at sea do it
They're so properly dressed
As Portnoy why didn't he do it
He was very repressed
Fat fleas in feverish fits do it
Television preachers at the Ritz do it
Let's do it
Let's fall in love

2.

Some folks before shoes and rice do it
Using every possible device do it
Let's do it
Let's fall in love
Marcel recalling past times did it
Mariners while sucking on their limes did it
Let's do it
Let's fall in love
What is Clark Kent on the prowl for
When he's wearing his cape?
And Batman puts on a cowl for
A clandestine escape
A. Graham Bell on the phone did it
Solemn Nietzsche sitting all alone did it
Let's do it
Let's fall in love

3.

Poirot who's no Provencal did it
Sweet Miss Marple straightening her shawl did it
Let's do it
Let's fall in love
Medieval monks just for Lent did it
Hammerstein with lots of sentiment did it
Let's do it
Let's fall in love
Big bumble bees with such class do it
When they're buzzing along
Rich T.V. preachers en masse do it
To the clamoring throng
Hermaphrodites maybe twice do it
People that you think are very nice do it
Let's do it
Let's fall in love

4.

Old Johann Bach yessirree did it
In between cantatas constantly did it
Let's do it
Let's fall in love
The Barrymores and the Lunts did it
Maybe God and Mary more than once did it
Let's do it
Let's fall in love
Some fussy prostitutes cuss men
And give nothing away
However, others like busmen
Like a nice holiday
Soft pussy cats when they must do it
William Buckley can but only just do it
Let's do it
Let's fall in love

5.

Great men in each former age did it
Lady Chatterley on every page did it
Let's do it
Let's fall in love
Fat Santa Claus in the snow does it
With all the little elves he – ho, ho, ho – does it
Let's do it
Let's fall in love
Miss Murdoch in every book does it
And she's very profound
But Sherlock Holmes says one look does it
If your logic is sound
And Casanova you bet did it
With absolutely everyone he met did it
Let's do it
Let's fall in love

"My Favorite Things"

Rodgers and Hammerstein

Comfy old slippers
And Christmas trees lit up,
Old broken zippers
And babies that spit up,
W. Bush when the chapel bell chimes -
These are a few of my favorite rhymes.
Jesus and Moses
And outlawing faggots,
Donald god knows is
Corrupter than maggots.
Reagan did things no one thinks of crimes.
These are some more of my favorite rhymes.
Jimmy Swaggart
In Manhattan
Kept a rendezvous.
With only the Bible beside him in bed,
The Rapture was just a Screw.

"All That Jazz"

Kander and Ebb

I know a low down dive that's just a walk from here
And all that jazz
Where all the men are friendly but they're insincere
And all that jazz
Where the emotion's shallow but the passion's deep
The men are most expensive but their talk is cheap
It's kinda nice to hear, it puts me right to sleep
And all that jazz

It's got a trumpet player with a burned out brain
And all that jazz
The drummer can't feel anything except cocaine
And all that jazz
The fiddle player's face expresses great disdain
Because his momma says that he is half insane
But when he plays his fiddle he can feel no pain
And all that jazz

There's not a goddamned thing to build your hopes upon
And all that jazz
I'm gonna cuddle up, I'm gonna carry on
And all that jazz
You'll see some silhouettes upon the purple glass
As someone plants a kiss upon a lady's ass
So if your nose is blue, then I suggest you pass
And all that jazz

"The Blue Room"

Rodgers & Hart

Down at the harbor
Each rat sees his barber,
And every mouse sweeps out her house
When they hear that the fleet is in.
Silent half-fish males
Just say, "Call us Ishmaels"
And grouchy louses cease to grouse
When they hear someone sweet is in.
Lovely ladies of the evening
Come out in the daytime.
It's April and May time.
They give it away.
Sailors and swabbies
And whalers and gobbies
All flex their pecs and hit the decks.
The indiscreet petite is in.

"Manhattan"

Rodgers & Hart

Keep your roach-infested flat in
What is known as old Manhattan.
We have an act
Sure to attract.
We'll play places lost in thickets,
Little bergs. We've got our tickets.
Hear Hackensack
Calling us back!
We'll do Dinuba.
I'll play my tuba,
You your flute.
And we will look so cute
When we just stand and toot
Folks will root.
I have a notion
We'll set old Goshen
On its ear
If we speak loud and clear
And if we are sincere.
Have a beer!
If Gotham offers a better fee,
The more provincial's for you and me.
Goodbye Manhattan!
We're going to climb a tree.

"Bewitched"

Rodgers & Hart

All of us are understudies,
Been it for a hundred years.
We are understudy buddies,
Crying the same tears.
She's the diva. That God knows is
Why an understudy mourns.
They keep giving her the roses.
We just get the thorns.
But there may be
A chance that we
Will triumph as stars just the same as she.
Great things happen in the theater,
They say.
All day she eats.
I'll say she eats!
I may fiddle with the fillet she eats.
Great things happen in the theater,
They say.
She is chic,
And she's loaded
With both fashion and poise,
But her rings
Are corroded,
And her voice is noise.
In her gems
And diadems
She's drifting to sea in the river Thames.
Great things happen in the theater,
They say.

"Battle Hymn Of The Republic"

Julia Ward Howe

Mine eyes have seen the glory of
The coming of the Lord.
If you have a couple billion
And you feel a little bored
America's a country you can
Easily afford.
The Truth is up to you.

In the beauty of the lilies Christ was
Born across the sea.
You can lock up little children.
You can alter history.
Supremacists will love you. You'll have
Immortality.
And God is on your side.

Oh! "You can grab a pussy."
Global warming isn't real.
Mexicans and immigrants
Are underneath your heel.
Like Jesus you'll be persecuted.
Animals don't feel.
When you are a star!

You'll feel mighty as an eagle with
Your woman standing there.
She will be an angel to all
Children blond and fair.
As for dark complected ones, she
"Really doesn't care."
Porn stars cost you dear!

Mock the weak, your fans will
Imitate the things you do.
Coin a phrase too infantile for
People over two.
Watch the children die and claim
It's not because of you.
You did nothing wrong.

The Christians call you holy. You're a
Saint among your kin.
You gave an extra meaning to
The noble thought of sin.
More popular than Jesus! You're
A little God of Tin.
A prophecy come true!

Standing like a Titan
And indifferent to tears,
A brain without an equal
And a penis with no peers.
Never mind the children.
You'll be President for years.
Iran don't frighten you.

The Constitution's history but
Meaningless today.
Science is ridiculous and
Reason is passe.
Bigots made you President
And they are here to stay.
God bless the USA!

Rhymes

Everyone who writes in rhyme
Has to have a paradigm.
Whether it is a-b-a-b
(For example "maybe baby"),
Or whether it more loosely lies,
(For instance in "The Bridge of Sighs").
Or the pattern of the sonnet
(Which I cannot write, dog gone it!).
Sometimes rhymes are repetitious
And occasionally vicious -
Oh, there's nothing so invigorating as a little rape
By a motorcycle gang from which you can't escape
With six or seven passersby to stand around and gape.
Oh, there's nothing so invigorating as a little rape.
Or they can be clever, smart
Like the rhymes of Larry Hart -
I'll get brown and sunned un-
Less this town is London.
Though in my flat I boil tea
And entertain like royalty,
My life is just a riddle.
Don't play upon your fiddle.
I won't hear its squeak,
My spirit's weak.
And when he did the Latin Quarter,
Something can be said for Porter -
You're the fruit
That is in my yogurt.
You're the suit

On a Humphrey Bogurt.
Rhymes were once the talk o' fellers
Like the thrifty Rockefellers.
I do not like the present age.
Artless poets think they're sage.
And now at last it seems betimes
The world will be fini with rhymes.

Acknowledgments

"Let's Do It" (Audience; GARBA)
Rhymes (Light)

www.ingramcontent.com/pod-product-compliance
Lightning Source LLC
Chambersburg PA
CBHW050027170726
48282CB00025B/580
9788119228683